Inhalt

Tag 1	Numbers	4
Tag 2	Colours	6
Tag 3	Time	8
Tag 4	Summer holidays	10
Tag 5	Weather	12
Fun page		14
Tag 6	Body	16
Tag 7	Clothes	18
Tag 8	Family	20
Tag 9	Feelings	22
Tag 10	Hobbies	24
Fun page		26
Tag 11	Fruits and vegetables	28
Tag 12	Farm animals	30
Tag 13	Travelling	32
Tag 14	Days of the week	34
Tag 15	School things	36
Fun page		38

1   2   3   4   5
one   two   three   four   five

6   7   8   9   10
six   seven   eight   nine   ten

1 How many?

Wie viele?

t _____   t _____

s _____   f _____   s _____

2 Watch the video and sing!

One, two, three, four, five,
once I caught a fish alive.
Six, seven, eight, nine, ten,
then I let it go again.

Key: 165

Eins, zwei, drei, vier, fünf,
einmal fing ich einen Fisch.
Sechs, sieben, acht, neun, zehn,
dann ließ ich ihn wieder los.

3 Find 4 mistakes!

4 Match!

15 − 12 =	five	three	20 − 18 =
10 − 9 =	two	eight	45 − 40 =
2 · 2 =	four	nine	3 + 3 =
3 · 3 =	six	seven	2 + 6 =
70 : 10 =	ten	one	5 · 2 =

green
orange
white
pink
brown
blue
yellow
black
red

1 **Write in the correct colour!**

Schreibe mit der passenden Farbe!

blue   black   brown   green

white   yellow   pink   red   orange

2 **Which colour is it?**

 yellow   _yellow_ _____

blue   _____

white   _____

black   _____

red   _____

pink   _____

orange   _____

brown   _____

green   _____

3 Circle the colour!

Kreise ein!

 KFRTGHNRAPOL**RED**KNTRL

 WKFOVNGRMS**GREEN**ENIFL

 GROMPILK**BLUE**ROFSJEKWM

 REKMSJF**ORANGE**BROMMER

 PIKEJNSJF**PINK**MENKIMSAOD

4 Colour in!

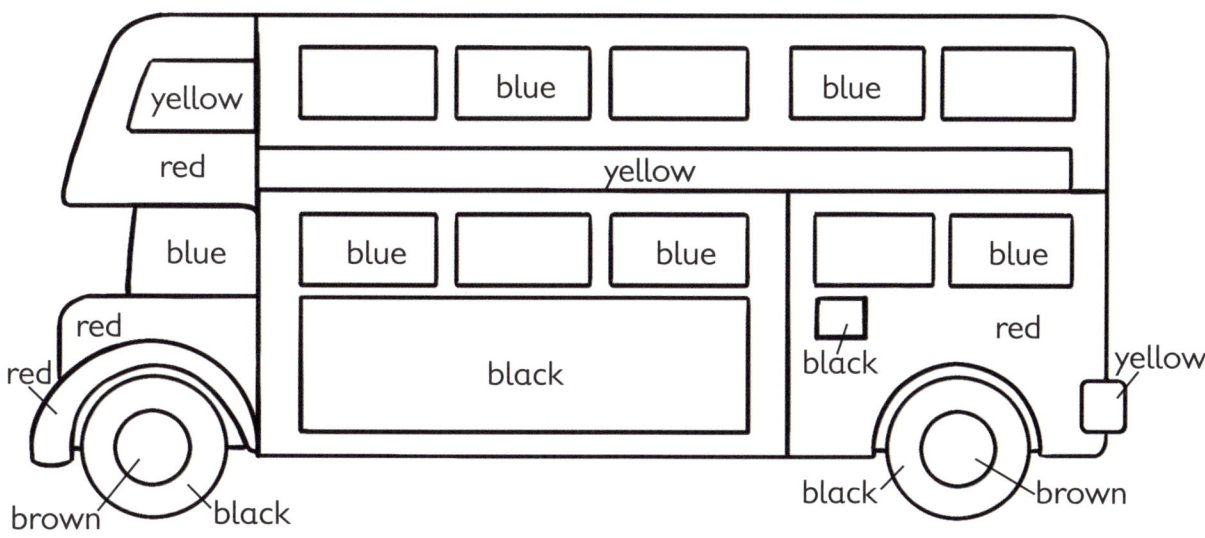

1 **What's the time?**

 It's 2 o'clock.

 It's 5 o'clock.

 It's ___ o'clock.

 It's ___ o'clock.

 _____ .

Wie spät ist es?

Achtung bei der Schreibweise! It's 3 o'clock.

2 **What's the time?**

It's eight o'clock.    It's seven o'clock.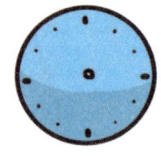

It's five o'clock.    It's four o'clock.

It's ten o'clock. 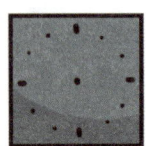   It's three o'clock.

3 Colour in!

Key: 237

 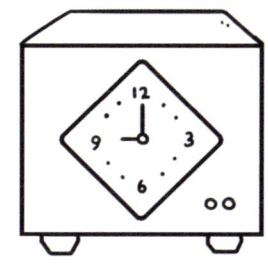 

4 Watch the video and sing!

Key: 497

Hickory Dickory Dock!
The mouse went up the clock.
The clock struck one.
The mouse went down.
Hickory Dickory Dock!
Tick, tock, tick, tock!

swimming   surfing   sailing   diving   fishing

1 Do you like …?

	yes	no
Do you like fishing?	☐	☐
Do you like surfing?	☐	☐
Do you like sailing?	☐	☐
Do you like diving?	☐	☐

Magst du …?

2 How many?

How many kids are swimming? _____

How many kids are fishing? _____

How many kids are surfing? _____

At the beach

3 Match!

sun

sandcastle

ice-cream

boat

fish

water

4 Colour in!

The sun is yellow. The sandcastle is brown.
The ice-cream is pink. The boat is orange.
The fish are green. The water bottle is blue.

1 Listen and colour the frame!

Key: 537

It's sunny.

It's windy.

It's raining.

It's snowing.

It's cloudy.

Male den Rahmen an!

2 Do the crossword!

3 **Find the words!**

r _____

s _____

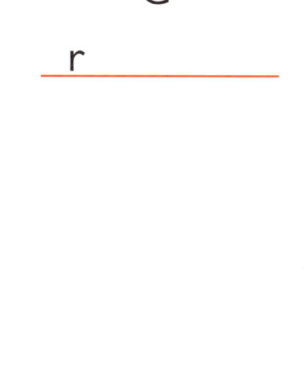

w _____

c _____

s _____

4 **What's the weather today?**

today = heute

Today it's _____ .

1 Let's do it!

★ Number the shirts!

★ Colour the shirts:
7 = blue	10 = green	2 = orange
8 = brown	5 = yellow	4 = pink

★ It's four o'clock.

★ It's sunny.

2 Roll the dice and colour!

Which ice-cream are they eating?

⚀	brown	🍫
⚁	pink	🫐
⚂	yellow	🍌
⚃	red	🍓
⚄	white	🌼
⚅	green	🍏

Würfle!

1 **Watch the video!**

🎧 **Sing along and move!**

Key: 571

Head, shoulders, knees and toes, knees and toes.
Head, shoulders, knees and toes, knees and toes.
And eyes and ears and mouth and nose.
Head, shoulders, knees and toes, knees and toes.

Bewege dich dazu!

2 **Point!**

🎧

Key: 572

Zeig hin!

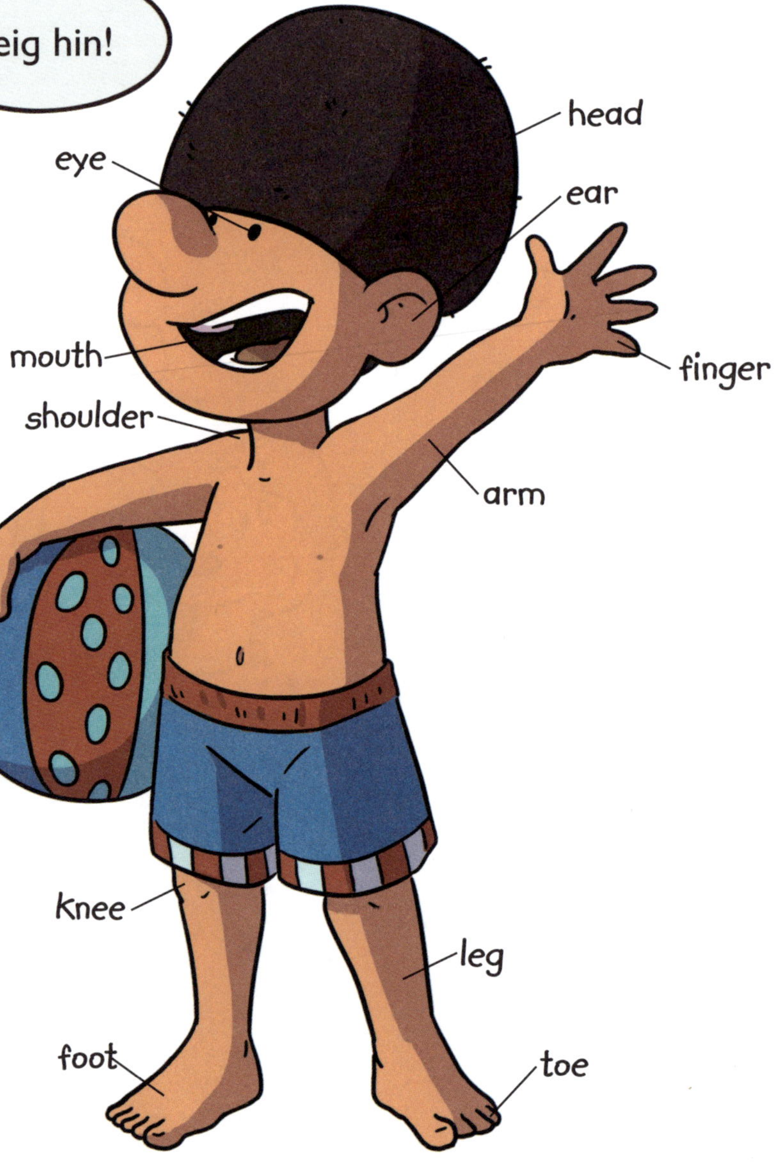

head

eye

ear

mouth

finger

shoulder

arm

knee

leg

foot

toe

3 Draw the monster!

It has seven ears.
It has five eyes.
It has six legs.
It has one toe.
It has four arms.

draw =
zeichnen

4 Write!

 e _ e

 _ o u _ _ _

 _ o e

 s h _ _ _ d _ _

 _ _ _ _ g _ _

 e _ r

1 **Find the words!**

K	H	N	O	G	J	N	T	J	T	X	I
I	E	E	S	V	N	Q	C	H	P	F	Y
U	G	I	K	C	V	D	R	E	S	S	T
I	J	E	A	N	S	R	T	G	Q	H	D
Y	G	H	A	Q	K	T	Y	I	J	C	F
K	X	V	R	P	U	L	L	O	V	E	R
S	R	H	A	T	V	V	Z	O	R	S	M
F	F	O	S	T	K	Q	N	V	G	H	I
J	F	Q	O	E	I	K	P	A	A	O	D
S	Q	V	C	L	Z	A	X	W	S	E	V
E	O	I	K	J	O	A	J	S	V	S	N
S	A	S	S	N	V	R	W	K	O	N	V

dress

jeans

shoes

socks

pullover

hat

2 **Write!**

T - s h i r t

3 **How many times can you write the word?**

Wie oft kannst du das Wort schreiben?

dress

hat

socks

1 Listen and point!

Key: 700

My name is Sherlock.
My mum's name is Mary.
My dad's name is Ben.
My brother's name is Willy.
My sister's name is Jenny.
My grandpa's name is Henry.
My grandma's name is Sue.

2 Match!

| Sue | Henry | Jenny | Willy | Ben | Mary |

| mum | grandma | dad | sister | grandpa | brother |

LÖSUNGEN

2

Liebe Eltern!

Mit diesem Ferienheft kann Ihr Kind die wichtigsten Inhalte des vergangenen Schuljahres während der Ferien wiederholen und festigen. Damit steigt es **bestens vorbereitet in die nächste Klasse** ein – ein klarer Vorteil für die weitere Schullaufbahn!
Die Inhalte werden dabei abwechslungsreich gemischt, mit spielerischen Elementen gewürzt und in 15 gut verdaulichen Tagesportionen angeboten, die die Kinder weitgehend selbstständig bewältigen können.

So können Sie Ihr Kind dabei unterstützen:

- Legen Sie gemeinsam drei Lernwochen oder 15 Lerntage fest und achten Sie auf die Einhaltung. Manchmal kann es auch hilfreich sein, eine Seite gemeinsam anzugehen!

- Mit den **herausnehmbaren Lösungen** können Sie die Ergebnisse eines Lerntages rasch kontrollieren oder das Kind selber überprüfen lassen.

- **Alle Lösungen** sind **in blauer Lösungsschrift** eingetragen, zeichnerische Lösungen eingezeichnet. Bisweilen gibt es neben der angegebenen Lösung noch weitere, individuell verschiedene.

- Zu guter Letzt: Die Reise durch die Aufgaben und Fun pages soll für Ihr Kind ein Vergnügen sein und Spaß machen! Dann ist der Lernerfolg am größten.

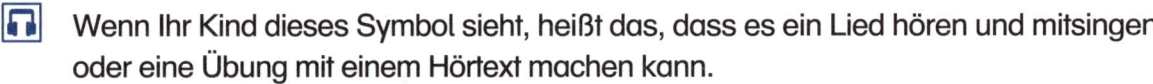 Wenn Ihr Kind dieses Symbol sieht, heißt das, dass es ein Lied hören und mitsingen oder eine Übung mit einem Hörtext machen kann.
Wenn Sie einen PC zur Verfügung haben, finden Sie die Lieder und Hörtexte auf:
http://ferienheft-englisch2vs.veritas.at
Wenn Ihr Kind die Lieder und Hörtexte auf seinem/Ihrem Handy anhören möchte, können Sie den Code neben der Übung mithilfe eines QR-Code Scanners (als Gratisapp verfügbar) einscannen.

Key: 123

Einen schönen Sommer wünschen Ihnen
Eva Kopinitsch und Michael Baker

Numbers

1	2	3	4	5
one	two	three	four	five
6	7	8	9	10
six	seven	eight	nine	ten

1 How many?

Wie viele?

two   ten

six   five   seven

2 Watch the video and sing!

Key: 165

One, two, three, four, five,
once I caught a fish alive.
Six, seven, eight, nine, ten,
then I let it go again.

Eins, zwei, drei, vier, fünf,
einmal fing ich einen Fisch.
Sechs, sieben, acht, neun, zehn,
dann ließ ich ihn wieder los.

3 Find 4 mistakes!

Finde 4 Fehler!

1 - ONE
2 - TWO
3 - THREE
4 - FOUR
5 - LIVE

6 - SIG
7 - TWO
8 - EIGHT
9 - NINE
10 - ONE

Verbinde!

4 Match!

15 − 12 = 3   three   20 − 18 = 2
   five
10 − 9 = 1   eight   45 − 40 = 5
   two
2 · 2 = 4   nine   3 + 3 = 6
   four
3 · 3 = 9   seven   2 + 6 = 8
   six
70 : 10 = 7   one   5 · 2 = 10
   ten

Colours

green   orange   white
pink   brown   blue
yellow   black   red

1 Write in the correct colour!

Schreibe mit der passenden Farbe!

blue   black   brown   green
white   yellow   pink   red   orange

2 Which colour is it?

yellow — yellow   pink — pink
blue — blue   orange — orange
white — white   brown — brown
black — black   green — green
red — red

3 Circle the colour!

Kreise ein!

KFRTGHNRAPOL**RED**KNTRL

WKFOVNGRMS**GREEN**ENIFL

GROMPILK**BLUE**ROFSJEKWM

REKMSJF**ORANGE**BROMMER

PIKEJNSJF**PINK**MENKIMSAOD

4 Colour in!

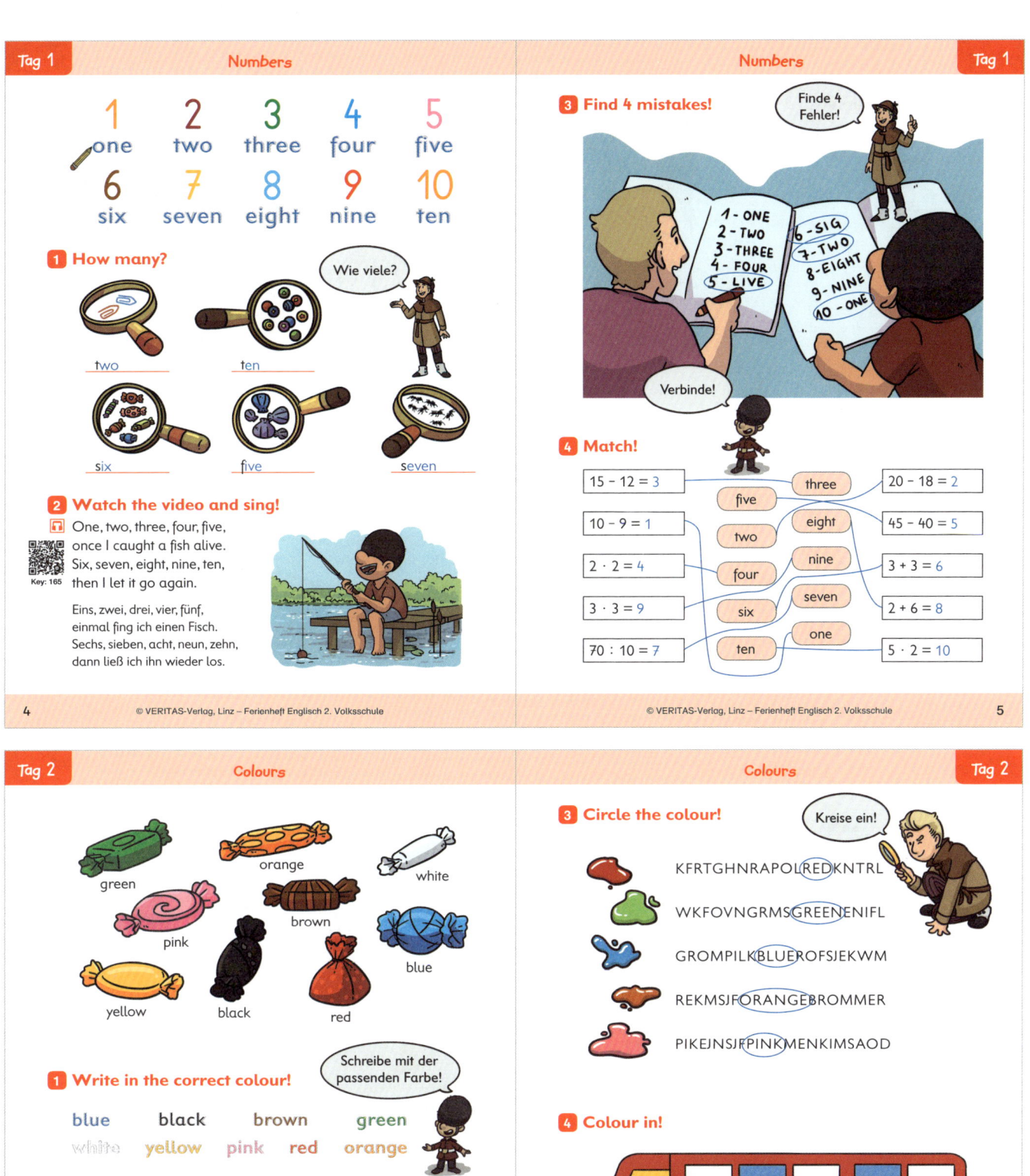

1 What's the time?

It's 2 o'clock.

It's 5 o'clock.

It's _6_ o'clock.

It's _9_ o'clock.

It's 1 o'clock.

Wie spät ist es?

Achtung bei der Schreibweise! It's 3 o'clock.

2 What's the time?

It's eight o'clock.

It's seven o'clock.

It's five o'clock.

It's four o'clock.

It's ten o'clock.

It's three o'clock.

3 Colour in!

Key: 237

4 Watch the video and sing!

Key: 497

Hickory Dickory Dock!
The mouse went up the clock.
The clock struck one.
The mouse went down.
Hickory Dickory Dock!
Tick, tock, tick, tock!

swimming   surfing   sailing   diving   fishing

1 Do you like ...?

individuelle Lösung

	yes	no
Do you like fishing?	☐	☐
Do you like surfing?	☐	☐
Do you like sailing?	☐	☐
Do you like diving?	☐	☐

Magst du …?

2 How many?

How many kids are swimming?   _8_

How many kids are fishing?   _4_

How many kids are surfing?   _3_

At the beach

3 Match!

sun

sandcastle

ice-cream

boat

fish

water

4 Colour in!

The sun is yellow.
The ice-cream is pink.
The fish are green.

The sandcastle is brown.
The boat is orange.
The water bottle is blue.

1 Listen and colour the frame!

Key: 537

It's sunny.  It's windy.  It's raining.

Male den Rahmen an!

It's snowing.  It's cloudy.

2 Do the crossword!

```
  3       4
2 S N O W I N G
  U       I
1 R A I N I N G
  N       D
5 C L O U D Y   Y
```

3 Find the words!

raining

snowing    windy

cloudy    sunny

4 What's the weather today?

individuelle Lösung

today = heute

Today it's _____.

ten
5
five
eight
seven
two
four

1 Let's do it!

★ Number the shirts!

★ Colour the shirts:
7 = blue   10 = green   2 = orange
8 = brown   5 = yellow   4 = pink

★ It's four o'clock.

★ It's sunny.

2 Roll the dice and colour!

Which ice-cream are they eating?

individuelle Lösung

brown
pink
yellow
red
white
green

Würfle!

1 Watch the video!
1 Sing along and move!

Key: 571

Head, shoulders, knees and toes, knees and toes.
Head, shoulders, knees and toes, knees and toes.
And eyes and ears and mouth and nose.
Head, shoulders, knees and toes, knees and toes.

Bewege dich dazu!

2 Point!

Zeig hin!

Key: 572

head
eye
ear
mouth
shoulder
finger
arm
knee
leg
foot
toe

---

3 Draw the monster!

It has seven ears.
It has five eyes.
It has six legs.
It has one toe.
It has four arms.

individuelle Lösung, zum Beispiel:

draw = zeichnen

4 Write!

e y e   m o u t h

t o e   s h o u l d e r

f i n g e r   e a r

shoes   socks
dress   T-shirt   hat
jeans   pullover

1 Find the words!

K	H	N	O	G	J	N	T	J	T	X	I
I	E	E	S	V	N	Q	C	H	P	F	Y
U	G	I	K	C	V	D	R	E	S	S	T
I	J	E	A	N	S	R	T	G	Q	H	D
Y	G	H	A	Q	K	T	Y	I	J	C	F
K	X	V	R	P	U	L	L	O	V	E	R
S	R	H	A	T	V	V	Z	O	R	S	M
F	F	O	S	T	K	Q	N	V	G	H	I
J	F	Q	O	E	I	K	P	A	A	O	D
S	Q	V	C	L	Z	A	X	W	S	E	V
E	O	I	K	J	O	A	J	S	V	S	N
S	A	S	S	N	V	R	W	K	O	N	V

dress
jeans
shoes
socks
pullover
hat

---

2 Write!

T - s h i r t

h a t   p u l l o v e r

s h o e s   d r e s s

j e a n s   s o c k s

3 How many times can you write the word?

Wie oft kannst du das Wort schreiben?

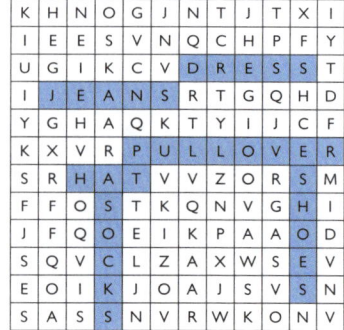

1 Listen and point!

Key: 700

grandma   grandpa   mum   dad

sister   Sherlock   brother

My name is Sherlock.
My mum's name is Mary.
My dad's name is Ben.
My brother's name is Willy.
My sister's name is Jenny.
My grandpa's name is Henry.
My grandma's name is Sue.

2 Match!

Sue	Henry	Jenny	Willy	Ben	Mary

mum	grandma	dad	sister	grandpa	brother

3 Who is it?

Wer ist es?

wear = tragen, anhaben

I am wearing a green dress.	grandma
I am wearing blue socks.	dad
I am wearing a brown hat.	grandpa
I am wearing a red pullover.	sister
I am wearing yellow shoes.	brother
I am wearing black jeans.	mum

4 Write and draw!   individuelle Lösung

My family

My name is _____.
My mum's name is _____.
My dad's name is _____.
My sister's / brother's name is _____.
My sister's / brother's name is _____.
My sister's / brother's name is _____.

How are you feeling?

1 Match the picture with the feeling!

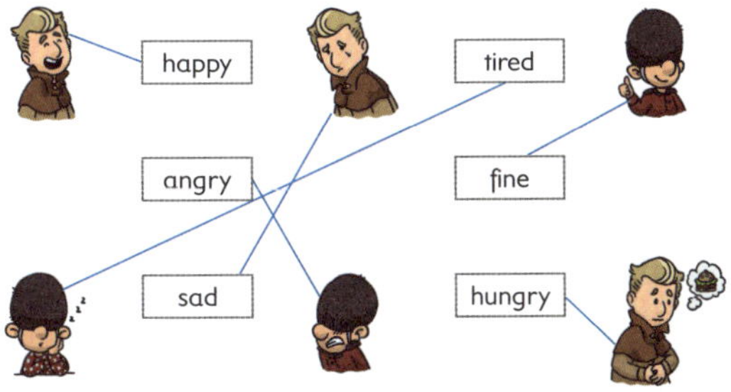

happy   tired   angry   fine   sad   hungry

2 True or false?

	T	F
happy	☒	☐
angry	☐	☒
sad	☒	☐
tired	☒	☐
fine	☐	☒
hungry	☐	☒

3 Find the match and colour!

hap	gry
an	ne
fi	py

s	gry
tir	ad
hun	ed

4 Circle the words!

happy   sad   hungry   tired   fine

Sherlock and Gary have lots of hobbies.

 4

 2

 1

 5

 6

 3

1 **Fill in the correct number!**

① playing football   ② roller skating   ③ riding a bike

④ skiing   ⑤ playing tennis   ⑥ listening to music

---

2 **What is missing? Draw it!**

Was fehlt? Zeichne es dazu!

3 **What is your favourite hobby? Draw it!**

individuelle Lösung

Was ist dein Lieblings-hobby?

"My favourite hobby is _____."

Fun page

1 **Snakes and ladders**

What you need:
a friend or your mum or dad to play this game with you

1 counter per player

a dice

How to play:
- Begin on the START square.
- The youngest player begins. Roll the dice.
- Name the picture: "It is an apple."

Ready, steady ...... GO!

- Snake square: If you land on a snake end you slide down to the head of the snake.
- Ladder square: If you land on the bottom of a ladder you can climb up to the top!

Fun page

2 **Help Sherlock to make a fruity hedgehog!**

What you need to make a fruity hedgehog:
- Some green grapes
- Some blue grapes
- A pear
- Some cocktail sticks (Zahnstocher)

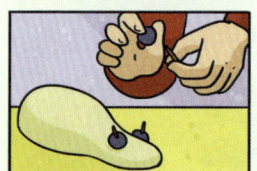

Step 1:
Wash all the fruit with water. Ask your mum or dad to help you with a sharp knife. Take the pear and cut it carefully in half. Put the pear on a plate.

Step 2:
For the nose and eyes take 3 blue grapes and carefully push a cocktail stick into the fruit. Now push the cocktail stick and the grape into the pear. The nose and eyes are finished.

Step 3:
Next you need to take lots of green grapes and carefully push the cocktail sticks into the grapes. Begin to place the grapes next to each other so they look like the spiky needles. Make one row after the other.

1 Match the fruits and vegetables!

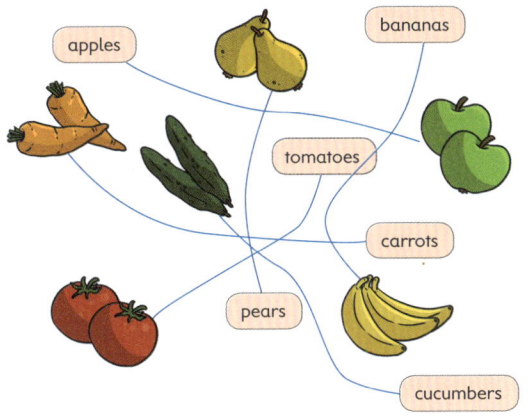

apples   bananas   tomatoes   carrots   pears   cucumbers

2 What colour are the fruits and vegetables?
🎧 Listen to Sherlock and Gary!

Key: 724

3 Help Sherlock and Gary to fill the shopping bag!
Draw!

Shopping list

5 tomatoes
4 pears
2 carrots
3 cucumbers
1 banana
6 apples

---

1 Watch the video and sing the song!
🎧 Old MacDonald had a farm

Key: 848

2 Number the farm animals!

① horse   ② duck   ③ mouse   ④ cat   ⑤ goose
⑥ cow   ⑦ pig   ⑧ sheep   ⑨ hen   ⑩ dog

3 Which animal is it? Help Sherlock!

h o r s e

d u c k

m o u s e

c a t

4 Animal noises: Tick the correct noise!

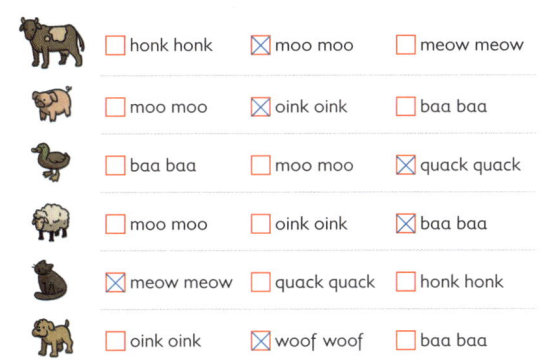

	honk honk	☒ moo moo	meow meow
	moo moo	☒ oink oink	baa baa
	baa baa	moo moo	☒ quack quack
	moo moo	oink oink	☒ baa baa
	☒ meow meow	quack quack	honk honk
	oink oink	☒ woof woof	baa baa

1 Listen and watch the video!

We all go travelling

Key: 867

2 Number the transport objects!

① train   ② bus   ③ truck   ④ plane
⑤ boat   ⑥ bike   ⑦ car

3 Colour the transport objects!

plane =   train =   car =

boat =   truck =   bus =

4 True or false?
Where are Sherlock and Gary going?

	true	false
Sherlock goes by bike to the park.	☒	☐
Sherlock and Gary go by train to London.	☐	☒
Sherlock goes by car to the supermarket.	☐	☒
Gary goes by bus to school.	☒	☐

5 What comes next? Write!

car	bike	car	bike	*car*	bike	car
boat	*bus*	boat	bus	boat	bus	boat
truck	car	*plane*	truck	car	plane	truck
train	*bus*	bus	train	bus	bus	train

1 Watch the video and sing the song!

Monday   Tuesday   Wednesday   Thursday   Friday   Saturday   Sunday

Key: 872

2 Word search: Find the 7 days of the week!

S	A	T	U	R	D	A	Y	T
F	E	U	I	M	T	E	C	H
R	X	E	S	O	P	H	Z	U
I	D	S	U	N	D	A	Y	R
D	P	D	Q	D	O	E	N	S
A	F	A	C	A	K	Y	B	D
Y	M	Y	U	Y	B	G	W	A
W	E	D	N	E	S	D	A	Y
A	F	Z	R	G	X	T	L	P

THE DAYS OF THE WEEK
Monday
Tuesday
Wednesday
Thursday
Friday
Saturday
Sunday

3 Which day is missing?

Monday   *Tuesday*   Wednesday

Friday   Saturday   Sunday

Tuesday   Wednesday   *Thursday*

4 Listen and number the pictures!

Sherlock and Gary are having a busy week.

Key: 882

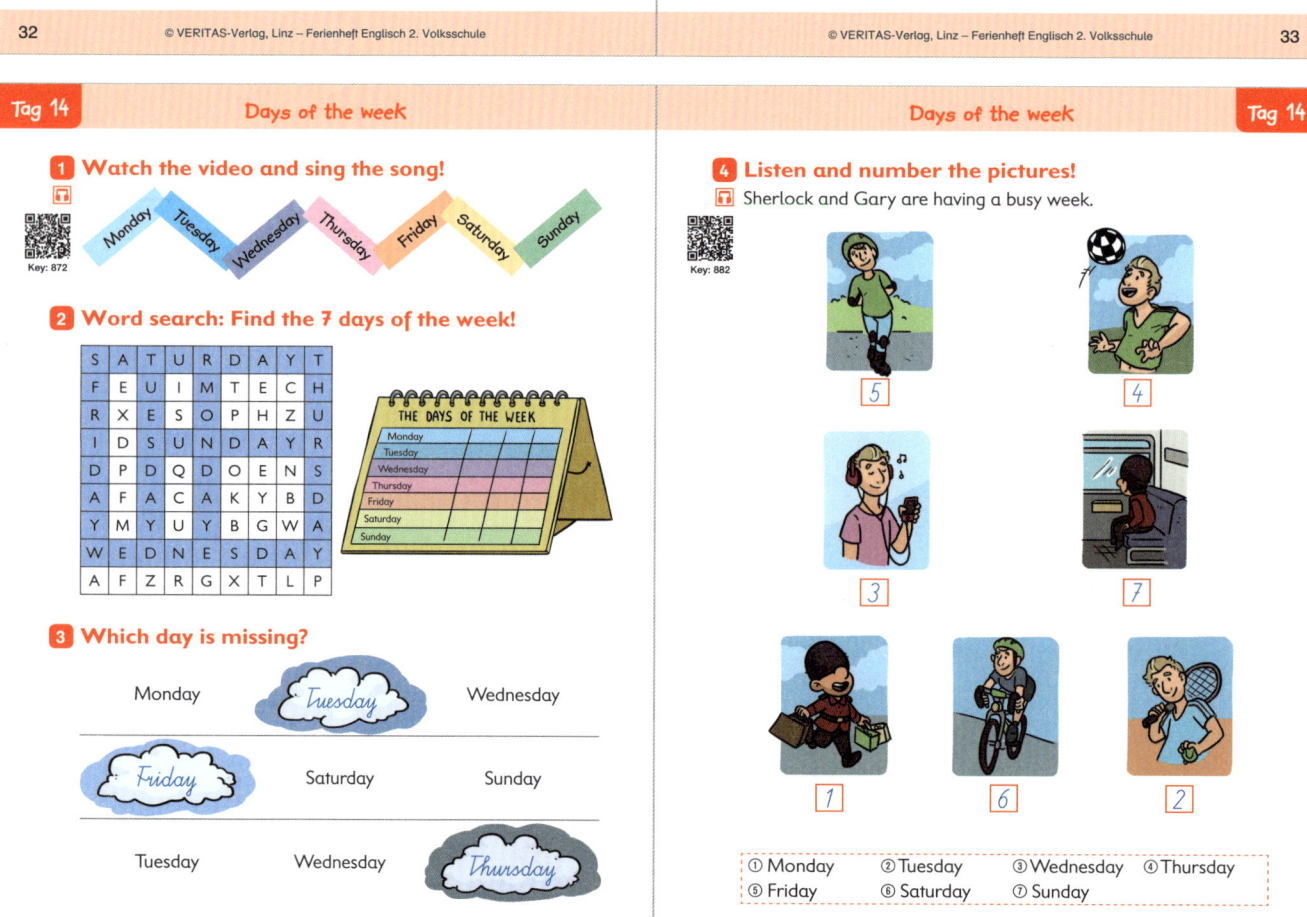

① Monday   ② Tuesday   ③ Wednesday   ④ Thursday
⑤ Friday   ⑥ Saturday   ⑦ Sunday

1 Match and colour the school things!

BOOK
PENCIL
PEN
RUBBER
CHAIR
PENCIL CASE
SHARPENER
DESK

2 Can you find the words?

```
        P
        E
  P E N C I L        R     D
        I            U     E
        L            B     S
  P     C        B  O  O  K
  E     A            E
  N     S            R
  C  H  A  I  R
  I     S
  L     E
```

Prepositions

Where is Gary?

in   under   behind   on

3 True or false?

	true	false
The pencil is ON the desk.	☒	☐
The pen is UNDER the chair.	☐	☒
The pencil sharpener is BEHIND the rubber.	☒	☐
The book is IN the pencil case.	☐	☒

4 Listen and colour the school things!

Key: 968

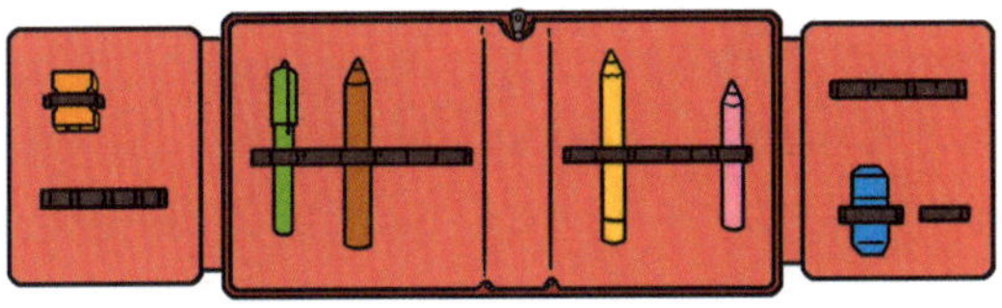

Fun page

1 Now it is your turn. How many English words do you know? Draw or write the vocabulary in the treasure chest!

Wie viele englische Wörter hast du dir gemerkt? Zeichne oder schreibe das Wort in die Schatztruhe!

individuelle Lösung

2 Colour one coin per word!

Male für jedes Wort eine Münze an!

GRATIS: ELTERN-INFOABO
FÜR GUTE NOTEN IN DER SCHULE!

Mit Ihrer Registrierung auf http://infoabo.veritas.at werden Sie regelmäßig über unsere **Sonderaktionen und Neuigkeiten** zum Thema „Gute Noten in der Schule" informiert.

Ihre Vorteile:

- **Aktuelle Informationen** zu Lernhilfen und Lernsoftware per E-Mail und Post erhalten
- **Nützliche Tipps** für Hausübungen, Schularbeiten, Schulrecht und Lernmanagement bekommen
- Persönliche Zusendung unseres Magazins für Lernhilfen und Lernsoftware **Eltern-Post** einmal pro Schuljahr
- Tolle Preise bei **Gewinnspielen**

Gleich registrieren unter http://infoabo.veritas.at

VERITAS Verlags- und Handelsges.m.b.H. & Co. OG
Hafenstraße 2a · 4020 Linz · Tel.: +43.(0)732.77 64 51-2280
kundenberatung@veritas.at

www.veritas.at

Gemeinsam besser lernen

VERITAS speichert Ihre Daten ausschließlich zum Zweck der Abwicklung von Bestellungen bzw. der Betreuung der KundInnen. Eine Weitergabe dieser Daten an Dritte ist ausgeschlossen. Rechtsform: Offene Gesellschaft (OG), Sitz: Linz, Firmenbuchgericht Linz, FN 190 f · UID-Nummer: ATU 23321402 · DVR 0658758 · Unbeschränkt haftende Gesellschafter: VERITAS Verlags- und Handelsges.m.b.H., Sitz: Linz, Firmenbuchgericht Linz, FN 86736 d; Franz Cornelsen Bildungsholding GmbH & Co. KG, Sitz: Berlin, Amtsgericht Charlottenburg, HRA 20764 B

3 **Who is it?**

wear = tragen, anhaben

Wer ist es?

I am wearing a green dress. *grandma*

I am wearing blue socks. _____

I am wearing a brown hat. _____

I am wearing a red pullover. _____

I am wearing yellow shoes. _____

I am wearing black jeans. _____

4 **Write and draw!**

My family

My name is _____ .

My mum's name is _____ .

My dad's name is _____ .

My sister's / brother's name is _____ .

My sister's / brother's name is _____ .

My sister's / brother's name is _____ .

How are you feeling?

1 **Match the picture with the feeling!**

happy   tired

angry   fine

sad   hungry

2 **True or false?**

happy   **T F**

angry   **T F**

sad   **T F**

tired   **T F**

fine   **T F**

hungry   **T F**

3 **Find the match and colour!**

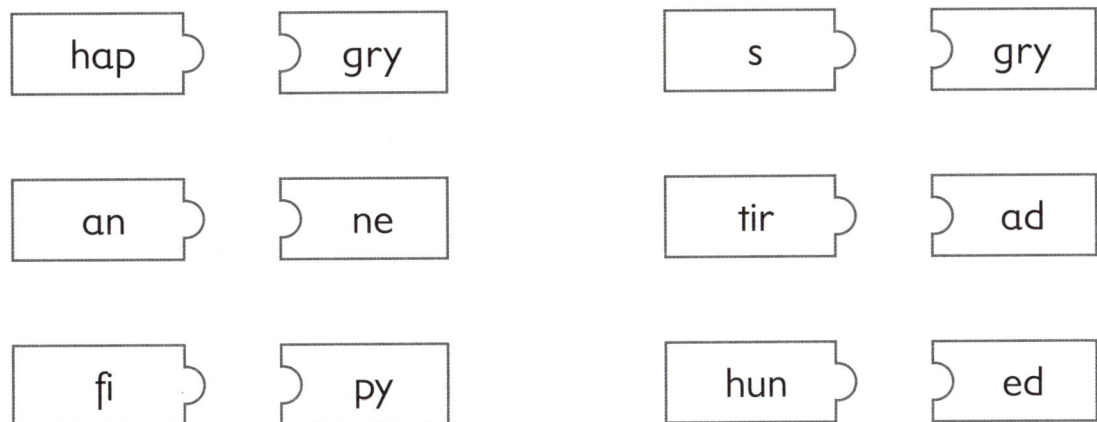

hap	gry		s	gry
an	ne		tir	ad
fi	py		hun	ed

4 **Circle the words!**

hscardowpspangrydflhpayuhapmfgnrhappymfteksyequmdnssadmrzifohappjifgltzjendaftreidfertiredgrppytzdfgumgryybasdyfinesfreradgfhuhungrysfgztujhjofinuopsmdethqainiredadesfg

Sherlock and Gary have lots of hobbies.

☐ ☐ ☐

☐ ☐ ☐

1 Fill in the correct number!

① playing football ② roller skating ③ riding a bike

④ skiing ⑤ playing tennis ⑥ listening to music

2 **What is missing? Draw it!**

3 **What is your favourite hobby? Draw it!**

"My favourite hobby is _____."

1 Snakes and ladders

FINISH

8

2

START

7

5

What you need:

a friend or your mum or dad to play this game with you

1 counter per player

a dice

How to play:
- Begin on the START square.
- The youngest player begins. Roll the dice.
- Name the picture: "It is an apple."

Ready, steady ...... GO!

- Snake square: If you land on a snake end you slide down to the head of the snake.

- Ladder square: If you land on the bottom of a ladder you can climb up to the top!

2 Help Sherlock to make a fruity hedgehog!

What you need to make a fruity hedgehog:

- Some green grapes
- Some blue grapes
- A pear
- Some cocktail sticks (Zahnstocher)

Step 1:
Wash all the fruit with water. Ask your mum or dad to help you with a sharp knife. Take the pear and cut it carefully in half. Put the pear on a plate.

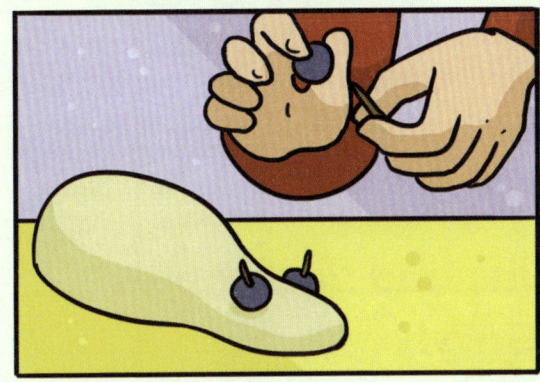

Step 2:
For the nose and eyes take 3 blue grapes and carefully push a cocktail stick into the fruit. Now push the cocktail stick and the grape into the pear. The nose and eyes are finished.

Step 3:
Next you need to take lots of green grapes and carefully push the cocktail sticks into the grapes. Begin to place the grapes next to each other so they look like the spiky needles. Make one row after the other.

1 **Match the fruits and vegetables!**

apples

bananas

tomatoes

carrots

pears

cucumbers

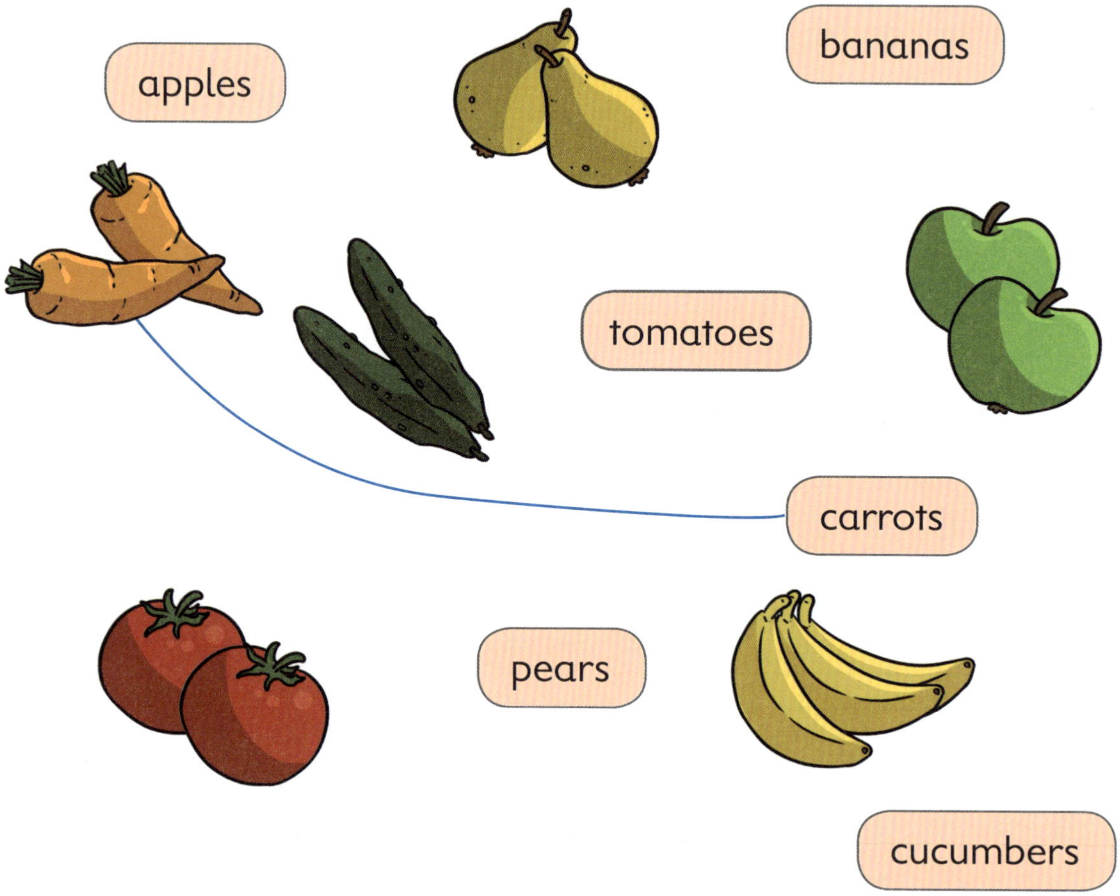

2 **What colour are the fruits and vegetables?**
🎧 **Listen to Sherlock and Gary!**

Key: 724

  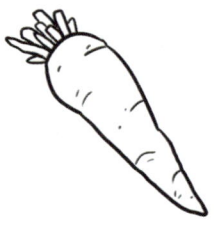  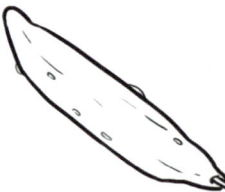

3 **Help Sherlock and Gary to fill the shopping bag! Draw!**

Shopping list

5 tomatoes
4 pears
2 carrots
3 cucumbers
1 banana
6 apples

1 **Watch the video and sing the song!**
🎧 **Old MacDonald had a farm**

Key: 848

2 **Number the farm animals!**

① horse   ② duck   ③ mouse   ④ cat   ⑤ goose

⑥ cow   ⑦ pig   ⑧ sheep   ⑨ hen   ⑩ dog

3 **Which animal is it? Help Sherlock!**

h ☐☐☐☐

☐☐☐ k

m ☐☐☐☐

☐☐ t

4 **Animal noises: Tick the correct noise!**

🐄	☐ honk honk	☐ moo moo	☐ meow meow
🐖	☐ moo moo	☐ oink oink	☐ baa baa
🦆	☐ baa baa	☐ moo moo	☐ quack quack
🐑	☐ moo moo	☐ oink oink	☐ baa baa
🐈	☐ meow meow	☐ quack quack	☐ honk honk
🐕	☐ oink oink	☐ woof woof	☐ baa baa

1 **Listen and watch the video!**

We all go travelling

Key: 867

2 **Number the transport objects!**

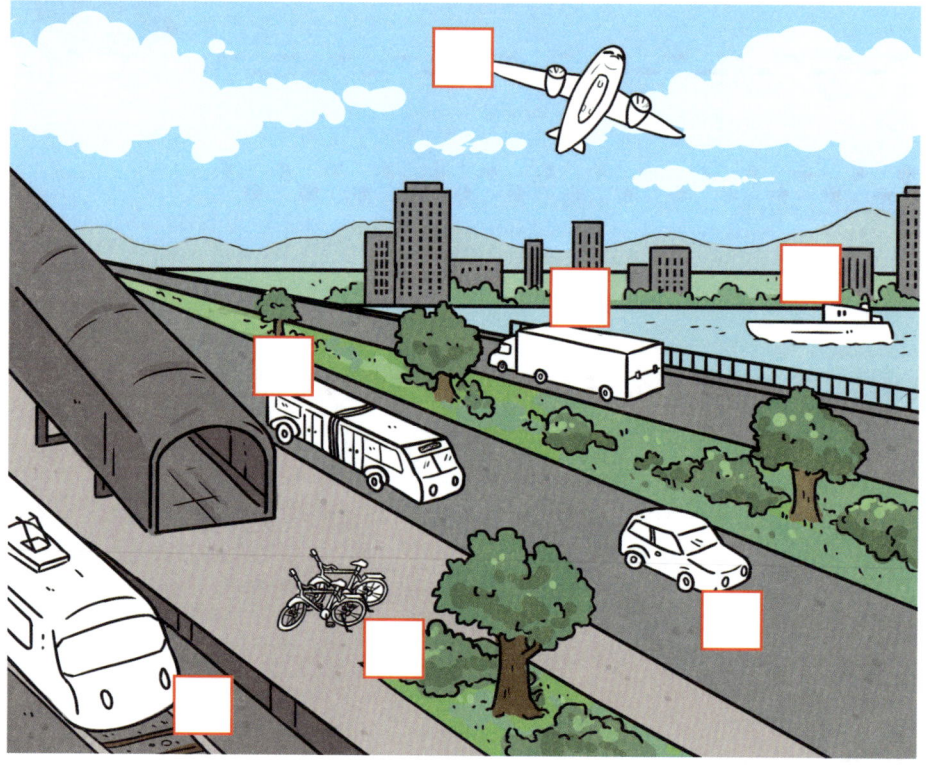

---

① train   ② bus   ③ truck   ④ plane

⑤ boat   ⑥ bike   ⑦ car

---

3 **Colour the transport objects!**

plane =   train =   car =

boat =   truck =   bus =

4 True or false?
Where are Sherlock and Gary going?

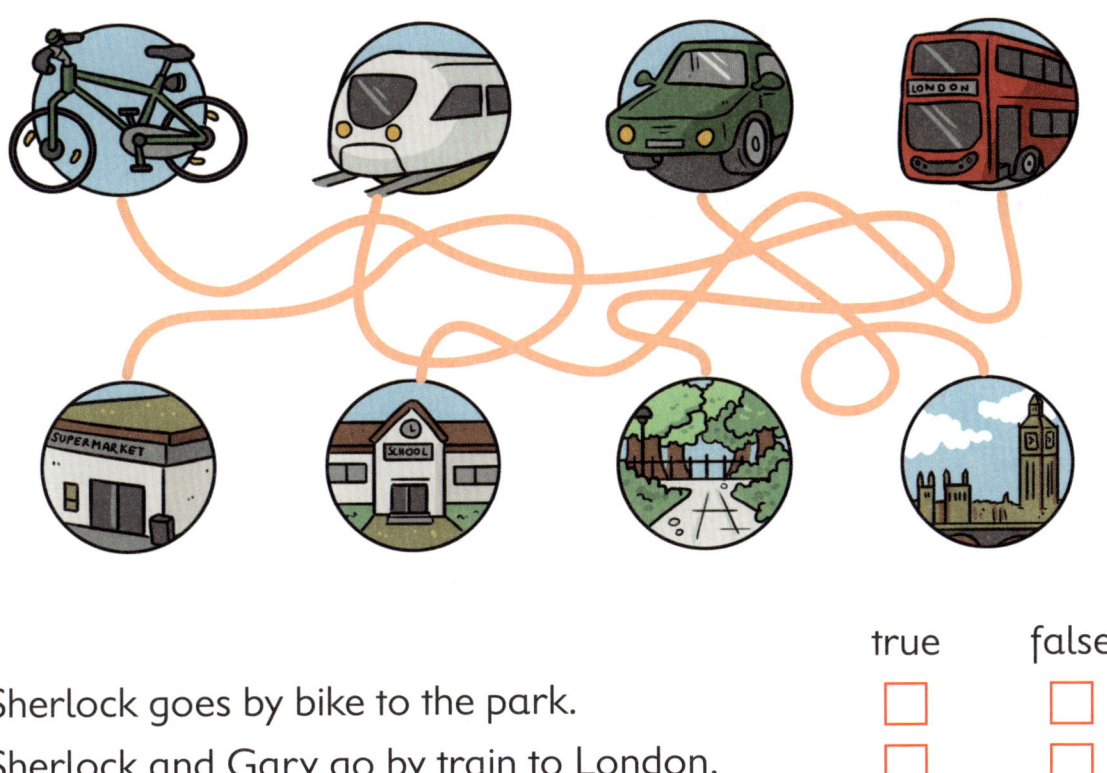

	true	false
Sherlock goes by bike to the park.	☐	☐
Sherlock and Gary go by train to London.	☐	☐
Sherlock goes by car to the supermarket.	☐	☐
Gary goes by bus to school.	☐	☐

5 What comes next? Write!

car	bike	car	bike		bike	car

boat		boat	bus	boat	bus	boat

truck	car		truck	car	plane	truck

train		bus	train	bus	bus	train

1 **Watch the video and sing the song!**

Key: 872

Monday Tuesday Wednesday Thursday Friday Saturday Sunday

2 **Word search: Find the 7 days of the week!**

S	A	T	U	R	D	A	Y	T
F	E	U	I	M	T	E	C	H
R	X	E	S	O	P	H	Z	U
I	D	S	U	N	D	A	Y	R
D	P	D	Q	D	O	E	N	S
A	F	A	C	A	K	Y	B	D
Y	M	Y	U	Y	B	G	W	A
W	E	D	N	E	S	D	A	Y
A	F	Z	R	G	X	T	L	P

THE DAYS OF THE WEEK

| Monday |
| Tuesday |
| Wednesday |
| Thursday |
| Friday |
| Saturday |
| Sunday |

3 **Which day is missing?**

Monday

Wednesday

Saturday

Sunday

Tuesday

Wednesday

4 Listen and number the pictures!

 Sherlock and Gary are having a busy week.

① Monday　② Tuesday　③ Wednesday　④ Thursday
⑤ Friday　⑥ Saturday　⑦ Sunday

Key: 882

1 Match and colour the school things!

BOOK
PENCIL
PEN
RUBBER
CHAIR
PENCIL CASE
SHARPENER
DESK

2 Can you find the words?

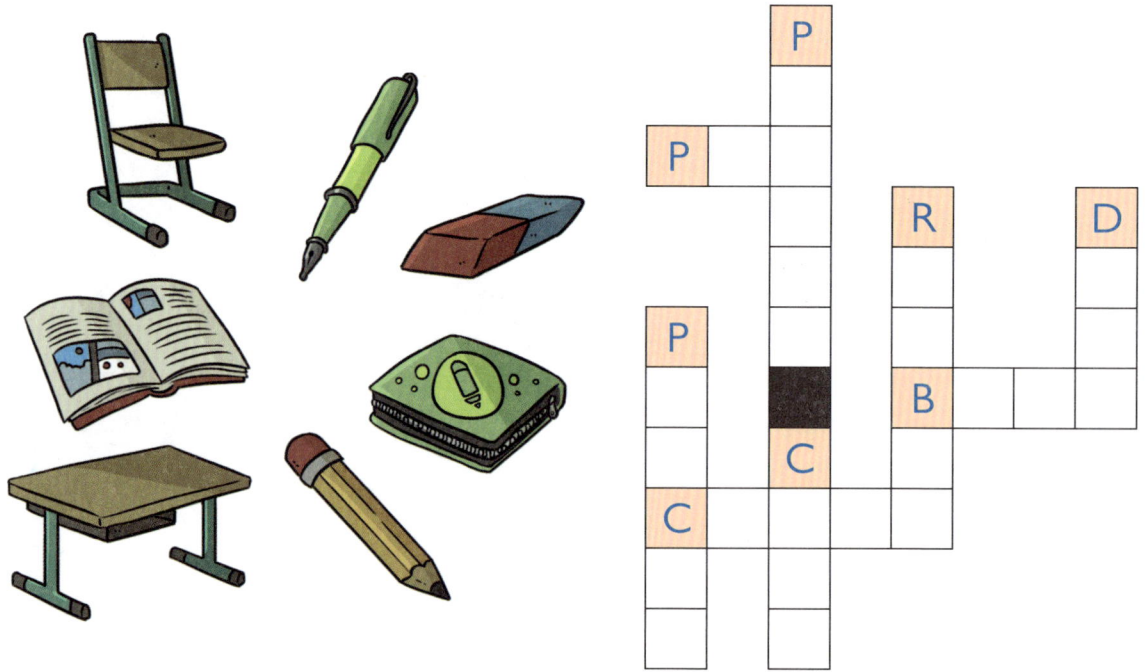

Prepositions

Where is Gary?

in   under   behind   on

3 **True or false?**

	true	false
The pencil is ON the desk.	☐	☐
The pen is UNDER the chair.	☐	☐
The pencil sharpener is BEHIND the rubber.	☐	☐
The book is IN the pencil case.	☐	☐

4 **Listen and colour the school things!**

Key: 968

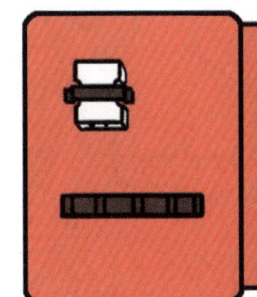  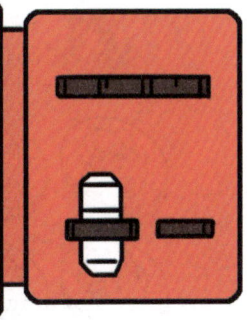